Just My Brother

Glynis Clacherty

Illustrated by Pippa Lugg

'Wake up, Maki! It's time to get up!'

Maki heard her brother Adisa, but she didn't want to move. She was warm, and she was sleepy.

Adisa was boiling water to make tea. He shouted, 'Maki! You're going to be late for school again!'

Maki took no notice. She wanted to go back to sleep.

Half an hour later she was still lying there. Adisa was angry. 'Well, I'm going without you!' he shouted, and slammed the door behind him.

After Adisa left, Maki slept peacefully. Then she suddenly woke up.

The weak winter sun was shining through the window on to her blanket.

'I'm late!' she gasped.

She knew that if the sun was shining through the window, she was late for school.

Maki ran as fast as she could along the road to school. She had dressed in a hurry. There was no time to eat. She had wrapped up a piece of dry porridge and taken it with her.

Her plastic school bag was banging against her legs. The stones in the road stuck into her bare feet. But she must not be late for school again!

Mrs Musi always shouted at her when she was late. Maki dreaded the teacher's shouting.

But Mrs Musi was not there yet. 'I am lucky today!' thought Maki. She slipped into her seat just as the teacher arrived at the door, with a pile of exercise books in her hands.

Maki smiled at Ethel, who smiled back and gave her a friendly pinch on the leg under the desk.

Maki couldn't concentrate on her school work. All morning she thought about Adisa slamming the door and leaving for school without her. He was very angry.

She felt so sorry that she had not listened to her brother. He tried hard to be a good head of the family.

Their mother had died three years ago. Since then, Adisa made tea every morning just like their mother.

Every day after school he helped Maki make the fire. When she had fetched the water, he helped her to heat it, and then to wash the clothes. He tried everything to get food for them both.

Yesterday Adisa had asked Mr Tembo next door if he could wash his car, even though this neighbour was always rude to him.

Adisa was the one who knew when Maki was missing their mother and feeling sad. Then he would sit very still with her on the back step. He held her hand until she did not feel so sad any more.

Maki knew that Adisa sometimes felt sad too. He would sit at the kitchen table, with his school books in front of him, but he wasn't doing any work. He would stare into space with a worried look on his face.

When he was like this, Maki would make him a mug of tea with many spoons of sugar and bring it to him.

Adisa was the one who wanted her to come with him to the club on Saturdays. It was a club for children whose parents had died, and it was run by Gogo Daphne.

Maki did not always want to go to the club. She wanted to walk round the village with her friend Ethel, greeting the other girls from school.

But Adisa said, 'We must go, Maki. We need people like Gogo Daphne, who will help us and give us advice, because we are alone.'

But the best thing about Adisa was that he helped Maki to remember their mother. When they finished their studying at night, they sat at the kitchen table and Adisa told Maki stories about their mother.

He reminded Maki how their mother liked Kwasa Kwasa music, and how she danced when she heard it on the radio. He reminded Maki how their mother called her 'Kwasa Kwasa girl' whenever she danced, too.

Maki could not clearly remember what their mother looked like, but Adisa knew and he reminded her.

When the school bell rang for break, Maki went to find Adisa. He was sitting under a tree with his friend, Victor.

Maki sat down next to her brother. He looked at her and smiled. She could see that he knew how she felt. He knew that she was sorry. Sorry for being late, and sorry that she had made him angry.

Maki unwrapped the piece of dry porridge she had brought from home, and broke off a piece for her brother.

He took it and said quietly, 'Thank you, Kwasa Kwasa girl.'

Let's talk

Do you know any children who live without adults in the house? (Perhaps you live alone with an older brother or sister.)

What are some of the problems that children face when they live without adults?

What help do children need when they live without adults?

How can children help each other when they live without adults?